P9-DIY-175

Dinosaur Puzzles

HIGHLIGHTS PRESS

Honesdale, Pennsylvania

Welcome, Hidden Pictures® Puzzlers!

When you finish a puzzle, check it off ☑. Good luck, and happy puzzling!

Contents

Cover illustration by Pat Lewis

Dinosaur Days

spoon

heart

needle

banana

open book

shoe

artist's brush

fish

ice-cream bar

pencil

lemon

slice of bread

sock

paintbrush

teapot

slice of pie

Art by Maggie Swanson

5

Tea for Two

slice of cake

wishbone

paint roller

boot

penguin

ice-cream cone

spoon

coat hanger

crescent moon

catfish

chili pepper

matchstick

ring

lamp

Art by Mary Sullivan

6

Dino Sock Hop

feather

pennant

carrot

party hat

barbell

light bulb

glove

sailboat

horseshoe

peanut

artist's brush

hatchet

bowl

banana

baseball

boot

ring

scissors

fish

Baby *T. rex*

slice of pizza

mushroom

tack

butter knife

bow

carrot

crown

lollipop

ice-cream cone

drinking glass

slug

trowel

mallet

artist's brush

kite

spoon

sailboat

hockey stick

pointy hat

bird

wishbone

party hat

canoe

ski

Art by Joe Seidita

Face to Face

ice-cream cone

banana

candle

sailboat

heart

bottle

mitten

glove

light bulb

bat

saw

shoe

snake

whale

9

Happy Birthday, Dinosaur!

crown

teacup

carrot

spool of thread

ring

crescent moon

arrow

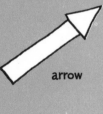
mitten

wedge of lemon

belt

ladder

saltshaker

beehive

lemon

eyeglasses

comb

lightning bolt

envelope

snowman

baseball bat

candy cane

ball of yarn

ruler

slice of pizza

fishhook

ladle

baseball

canoe

fish

hot dog

Art by Mernie Gallagher-Cole

11

Diving Dinos

dog bone

pencil

funnel

fried egg

flashlight

heart

wishbone

hat

Art by Patrick Girouard

12

At the Museum

bell

baseball bat

boot

snake

sock

drinking straw

needle

pencil

flashlight

carrot

envelope

toothbrush

slice of bread

Art by R. Michael Palan

Time to Eat

slice of cake

feather

eyeglasses

key

pen

tube of toothpaste

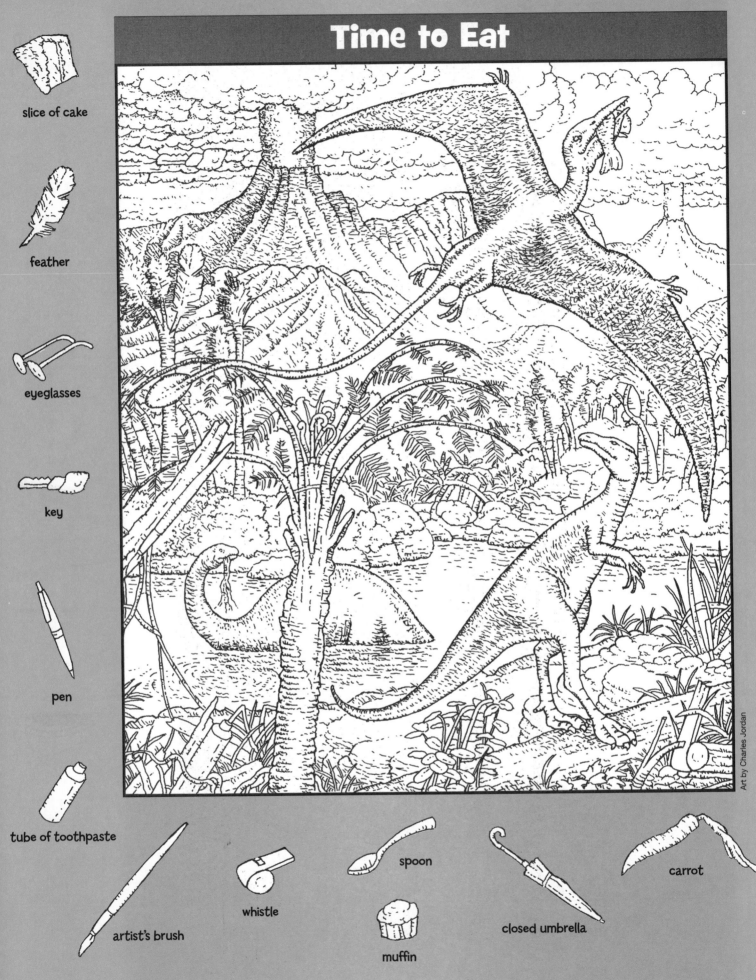

Art by Charles Jordan

artist's brush

whistle

muffin

spoon

closed umbrella

carrot

A New 'Do

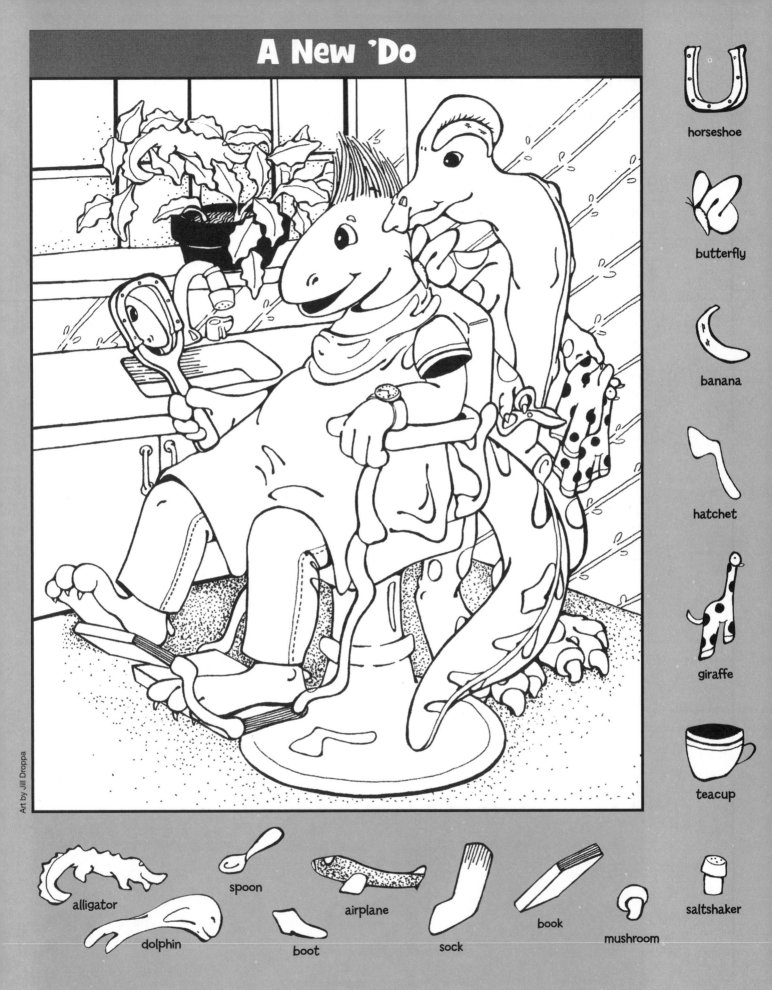

Art by Jill Droppa

horseshoe

butterfly

banana

hatchet

giraffe

teacup

saltshaker

alligator

spoon

airplane

book

mushroom

dolphin

boot

sock

15

Summer Games

crescent moon

bird

party hat

pencil

tomato

mitten

doughnut

heart

kite

slice of pizza

ruler

slice of pie

Art by Mernie Gallagher-Cole

17

Museum Marvels

teardrop

rocket ship

mushroom

broccoli

money

peanut

baseball bat

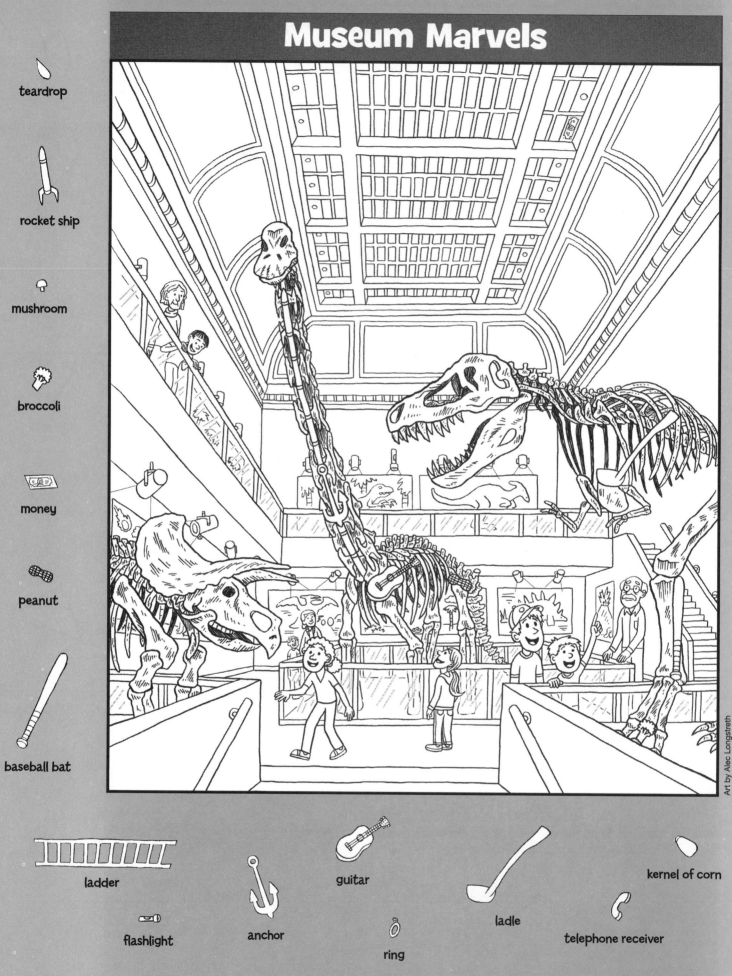

Art by Alec Longstreth

ladder

flashlight

anchor

ring

guitar

ladle

telephone receiver

kernel of corn

18

Prehistoric Pen Pals

crescent moon

golf club

candle

ladder

teacup

magnet

toothbrush

bell

ring

shoe

horn

bottle

saucepan

pennant

fish

Art by Mary Sullivan

Roar!

parrot

knitted hat

bathrobe

bell

hamburger

telephone receiver

car

book

mouse

Pilgrim's hat

bugle

roller skate

airplane

Art by Kit Wray

Baby *Apatosaurus*

Art by Joe Seidita

spoon

toothbrush

drinking glass

fork

shovel

elf's hat

ice-cream bar

wishbone

crown

mushroom

butter knife

lollipop

hockey stick

high-heeled shoe

cowboy hat

loaf of bread

carrot

bat

frying pan

slice of watermelon

tack

canoe

pointy hat

seagull

banana

bow

slice of pie

snake

boomerang

artist's brush

Jurassic Skate Park

mitten

fishhook

elf's hat

flag

boomerang

nail

feather

comb

vase

olive

paper clip

envelope

banana

tooth

ladder

fish

lightning bolt

crown

ice-cream cone

bowling ball

needle and thread

ruler

golf club

artist's brush

hairpin

carrot

hockey stick

crescent moon

worm

slice of bread

Styracosaurus

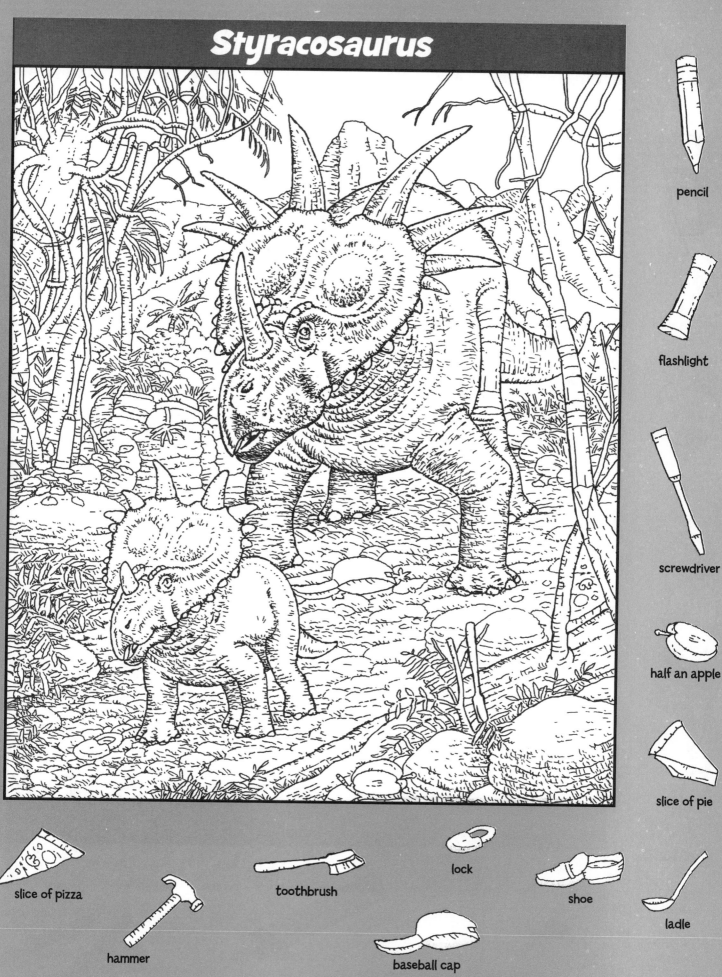

Art by Charles Jordan

pencil

flashlight

screwdriver

half an apple

slice of pie

slice of pizza

hammer

toothbrush

baseball cap

lock

shoe

ladle

23

carrot

ice-cream cone

balloon

sailboat

eyeglasses

bird

bell

roller skate

teacup

crown

snake

scissors

banana

Art by Tim Davis

Fossil Friends

toy top

pear

plunger

teacup

paintbrush

sock

sailboat

nail

needle

chili pepper

slice of pie

banana

toothbrush

carrot

feather

arrowhead

fish

caterpillar

Art by Janet Robertson

Dinosaur Slide

elf's hat

peanut

jelly bean

glove

ice-cream cone

hat

slice of bread

coat hanger

Art by C.A. Nobens

Just Hatched

musical note

pencil

crescent moon

mushroom

drinking straw

boot

bat

artist's brush

knitted hat

wedge of orange

fish

baseball cap

wishbone

open book

Art by R. Michael Palan

Going to the Museum

slice of cake

candy corn

light bulb

fish

harmonica

muffin

megaphone

ax

carrot

battery

rake

banana

flashlight

ladle

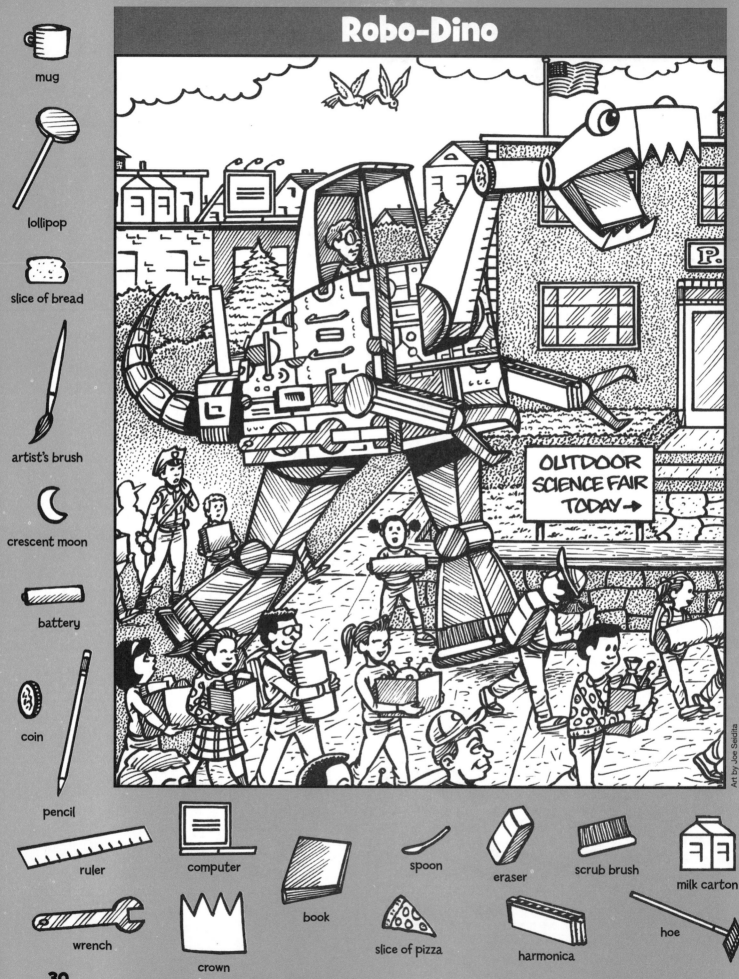

Horned Dinosaur

Art by Charles Jordan

golf club

pencil

pliers

ice-cream cone

artist's brush

mallet

feather duster

spoon

teacup

canteen

book

screwdriver

Underwater Dinosaur

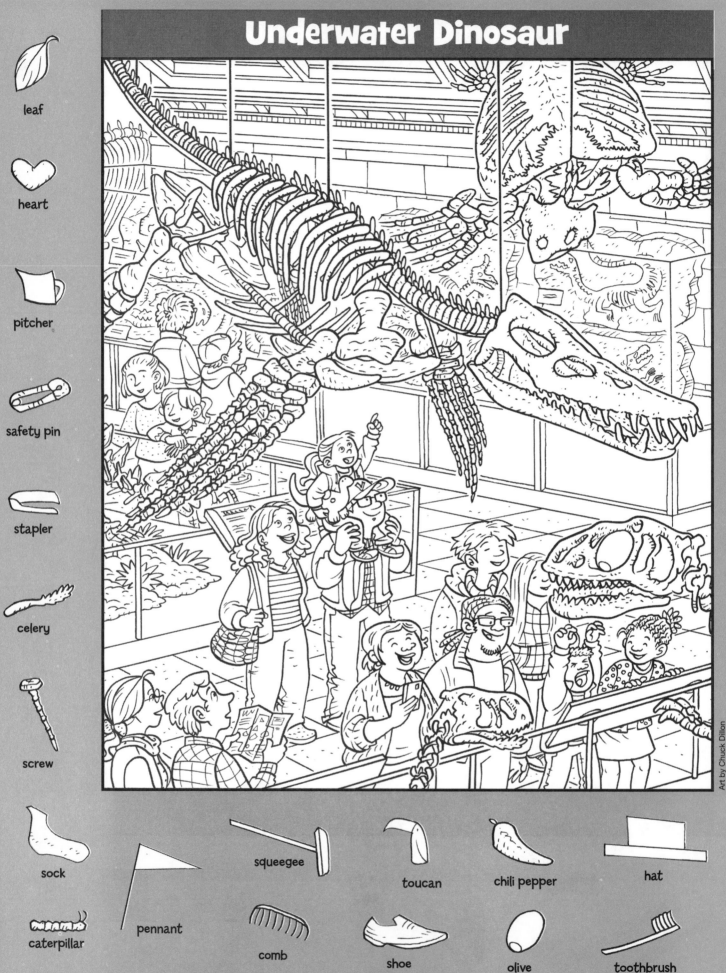

leaf

heart

pitcher

safety pin

stapler

celery

screw

sock

caterpillar

pennant

comb

squeegee

toucan

chili pepper

hat

shoe

olive

toothbrush

Art by Chuck Dillon

32

Dr. Katt's Lab

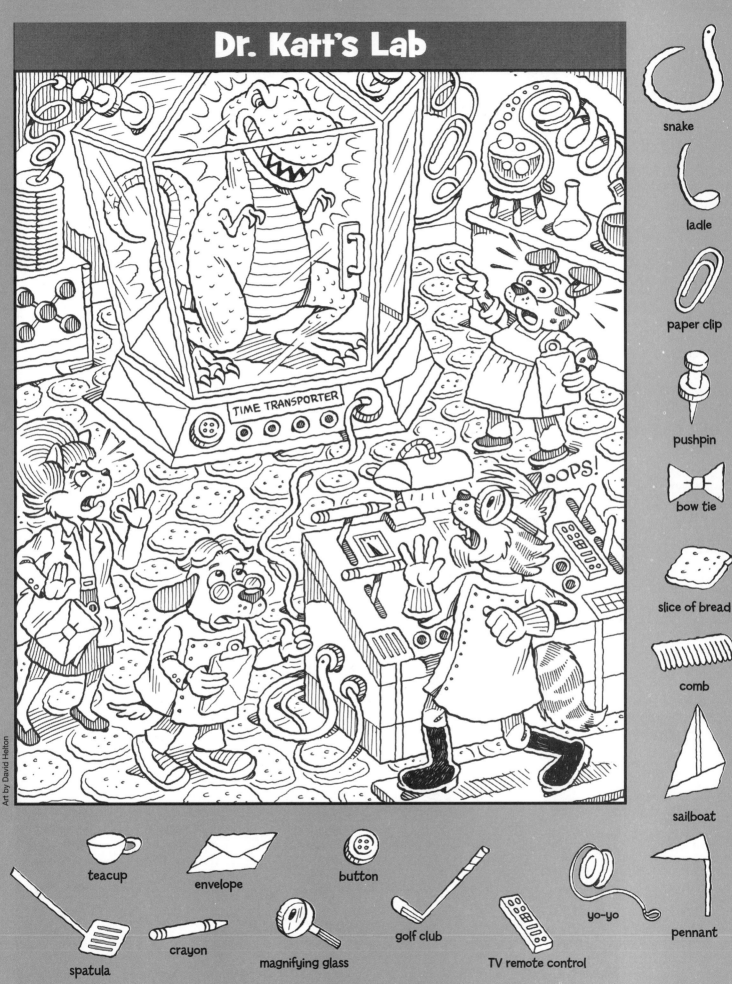

TIME TRANSPORTER

OOPS!

snake

ladle

paper clip

pushpin

bow tie

slice of bread

comb

sailboat

pennant

teacup

envelope

button

crayon

magnifying glass

golf club

TV remote control

yo-yo

spatula

Art by David Helton

Discovering the Past

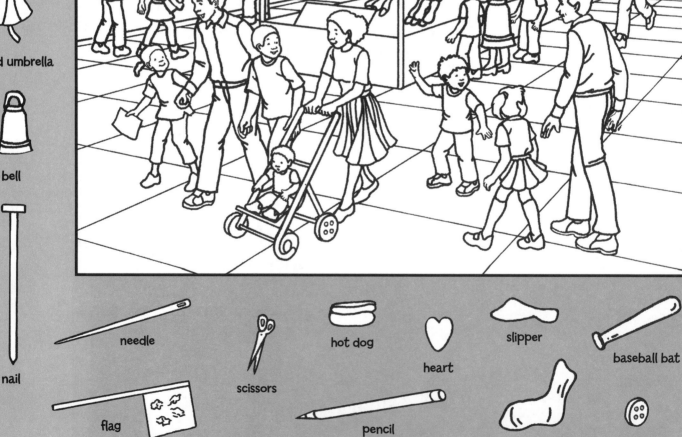

cane

candle

seashell

closed umbrella

bell

nail

needle

scissors

hot dog

heart

slipper

baseball bat

flag

pencil

sock

button

Art by Sally Springer

34

Game Night

spatula

candle

pencil

toothbrush

banana

sailboat

button

plate

pennant

slice of pie

envelope

feather

paintbrush

crescent moon

Art by David Helton

MOBY DICK

Baby *Pteranodon*

cornucopia

slug

ice-cream cone

spoon

carrot

pennant

bow

high-heeled shoe

butter knife

pointy hat

drinking glass

boomerang

hockey stick

slice of pizza

bat

sock

bird

wishbone

canoe

elf's hat

mallet

toothbrush

artist's brush

fork

snake

banana

sailboat

Art by Joe Seidita

Scooter Race

golf club

pen

tack

artist's brush

mitten

key

ladle

radish

spatula

slice of cake

toothbrush

banana

Art by Charles Jordan

Go, Team, Go!

envelope

pear

heart

light bulb

crown

pencil

Art by Sally Springer

car

teacup

fork

crescent moon

musical note

cane

Dino Dance-Off

sock

test tube

flashlight

trowel

key

hamburger

canoe

swim fin

fish

crowbar

boomerang

wishbone

needle

penguin

vase

belt

elf's shoe

glove

spool of thread

baseball bat

iron

tack

drinking straw

ladle

Art by Mark Corcoran

Dinosaur Air Show

glove

artist's brush

ruler

chef's hat

boomerang

button

mallet

horseshoe

fork

swim fin

wishbone

envelope

Art by Patrick Girouard

A Peek at the Past

tweezers

ghost

nail

screwdriver

ice-cream bar

banana

lemon

fishhook

fish

slice of bread

funnel

ice-cream cone

drinking glass

candle

glove

muffin

envelope

sock

mallet

hockey stick

fork

artist's brush

scissors

Art by Chuck Galey

flag

carrot

bowl

toothbrush

bell

hatchet

pushpin

wishbone

spatula

pencil

comb

45

Strike!

drinking glass

crescent moon

candle

egg

lollipop

snake

feather

canoe

scissors

carrot

needle

teacup

slice of pie

Art by Gary Mohrman

46

Baby *Allosaurus*

Art by Joe Seldita

banana

archer's hat

lollipop

boot

bird

party hat

spaceship

sailboat

cowboy hat

bowl

tack

whale

horn

canoe

jellyfish

butter knife

pointy hat

spoon

loaf of bread

surfboard

dragonfly

47

Dinner for One

ice-cream cone

feather

cinnamon bun

banana

pencil

slice of pie

Art by Susan T. Hall

bowl

slice of pizza

worm

eyeglasses

sailboat

toothbrush

button

scissors

cat

48

Amazing Artifacts

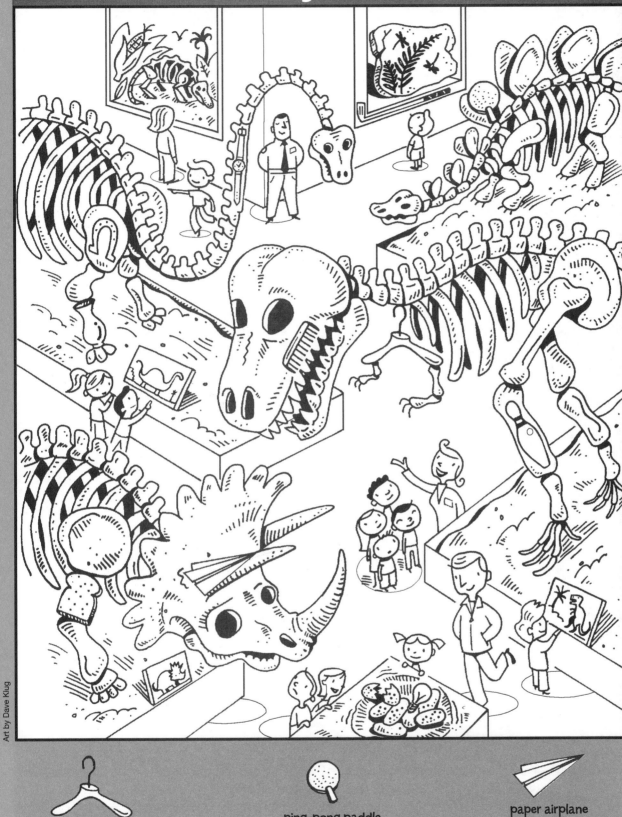

bowling pin

horseshoe

vase

ear of corn

wristwatch

light bulb

coat hanger

ping-pong paddle

paper airplane

golf club

slice of bread

comb

Art by Dave Klug

49

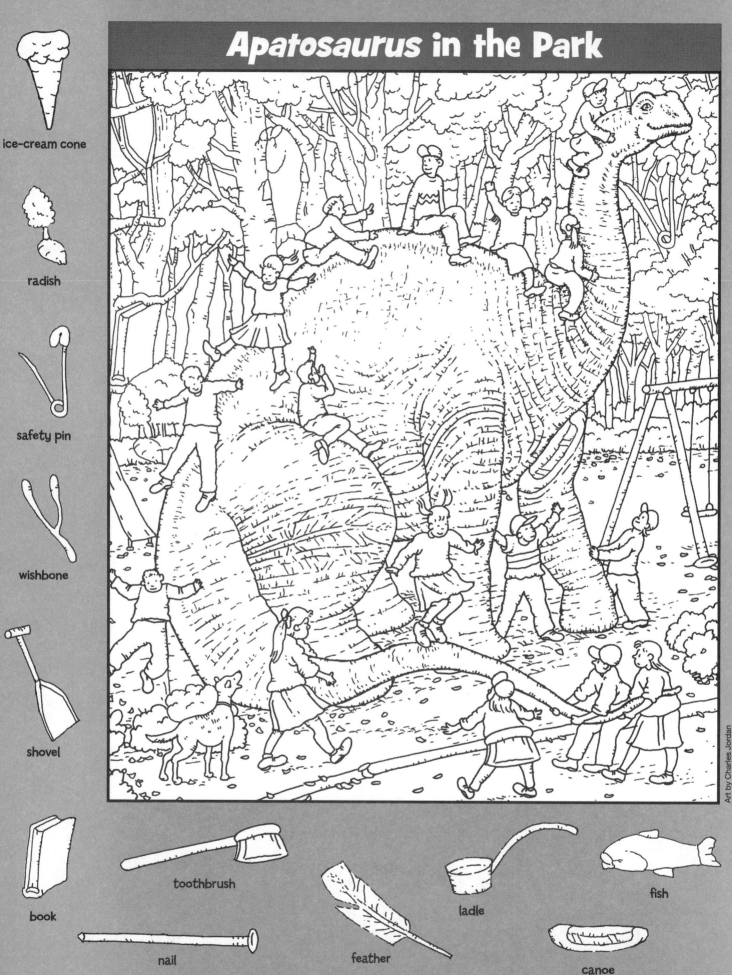

ice-cream cone

radish

safety pin

wishbone

shovel

book

toothbrush

nail

feather

ladle

fish

canoe

Art by Charles Jordan

Look What Hatched!

slice of pizza

rabbit

crescent moon

funnel

shoe

paper clip

boot

pennant

bowl

wizard's hat

boomerang

crown

pair of pants

Art by Cathy Copeland

51

wedge of lemon

seashell

lollipop

wishbone

heart

game piece

Prehistoric Party

slice of bread

flashlight

artist's brush

slice of pizza

comb

envelope

52

wedge of cheese

crown

magnet

tomato

pencil

mitten

toothbrush

doughnut

tennis ball

tooth

arrowhead

adhesive bandage

pipe

Art by Patrick Girouard

53

Dinosaurs at the Dentist

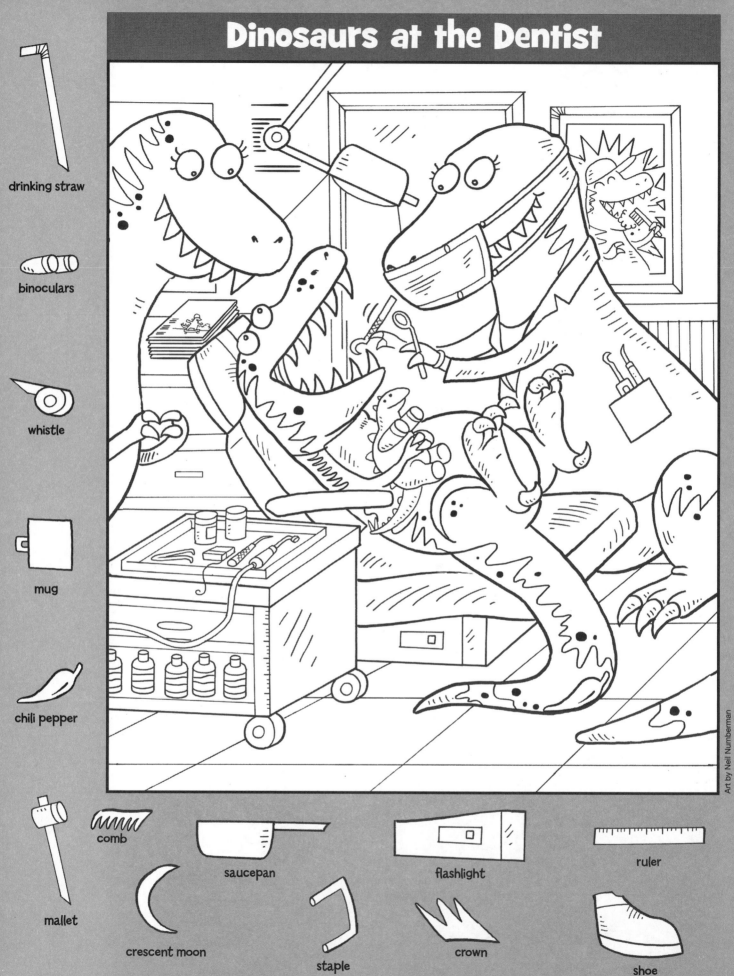

drinking straw

binoculars

whistle

mug

chili pepper

mallet

comb

saucepan

crescent moon

staple

flashlight

crown

ruler

shoe

Art by Neil Numberman

A New Discovery

tack

screwdriver

lock

funnel

lollipop

heart

artist's brush

sailboat

boot

ring

crown

slice of pie

needle

Art by Scott Brooks

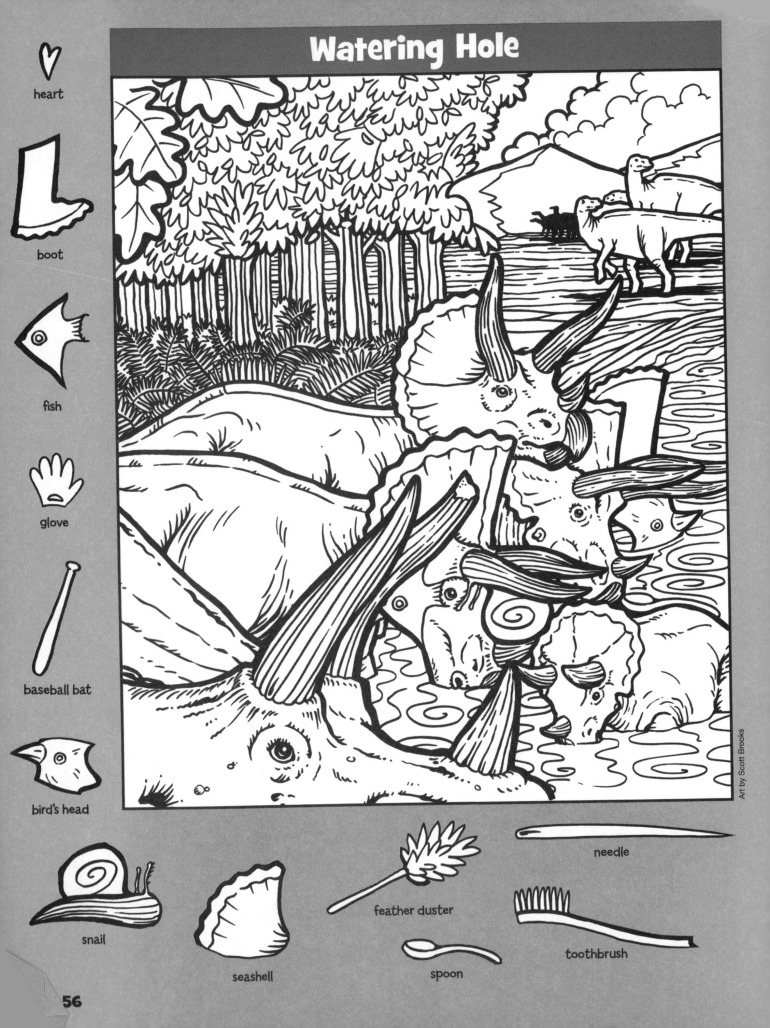

Watering Hole

heart

boot

fish

glove

baseball bat

bird's head

snail

seashell

feather duster

spoon

needle

toothbrush

Art by Scott Brooks

Lost Bones

tack

clover

radish

flag

party hat

ladder

ice-cream scoop

toothbrush

slice of bread

chef's hat

comb

spoon

pear

Corythosaurus Kids

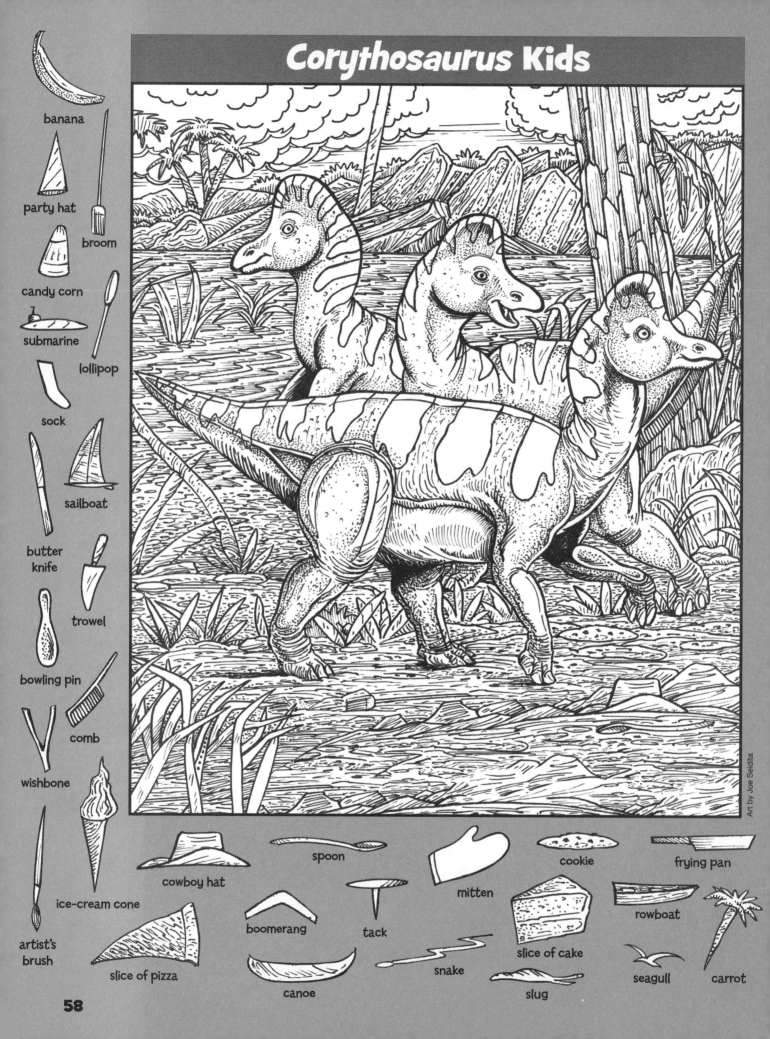

banana

party hat

broom

candy corn

submarine

lollipop

sock

sailboat

butter knife

trowel

bowling pin

comb

wishbone

ice-cream cone

artist's brush

cowboy hat

spoon

cookie

frying pan

mitten

boomerang

tack

rowboat

slice of cake

slice of pizza

canoe

snake

slug

seagull

carrot

Art by Joe Seldita

Dinosaur Jams

Art by Bart Castle

bell

mushroom

saltshaker

snowman

hammer

ladle

piece of popcorn

bat

toothbrush

wrench

pencil

spoon

boomerang

fish

cat

Dino Friends

trowel

crescent moon

vase

heart

crown

pennant

adhesive bandage

ring

mitten

olive

fish

boot

Art by Catherine Copeland

Museum Treasures

snake

leaf

candy cane

drinking straw

slice of pizza

comb

baseball bat

puzzle piece

banana

toothbrush

ice-cream bar

heart

key

kite

egg

wrench

pencil

flag

snowman

ice-cream cone

ruler

Art by Jennifer King Harney

Feeding Time

rabbit

scissors

duck

mug

dog's head

comb

stocking cap

crescent moon

bell

fish

ice-cream cone

sailboat

football

snake

turtle

caterpillar

Art by Patrick Coleman

62

Construction Crew

toothbrush

plunger

fishhook

drinking straw

ladle

top hat

diamond

pencil

domino

crown

flyswatter

flashlight

wedge of lemon

spoon

paper airplane

book

pitcher

spoon

ruler

envelope

snake

ULTRASAURUS

bat

pencil

butterfly

canoe

light bulb

pennant

Art by Ellen Appleby

Baby *Plesiosaurus*

ice-cream cone

mushroom

lollipop

crescent moon

mitten

ice-cream bar

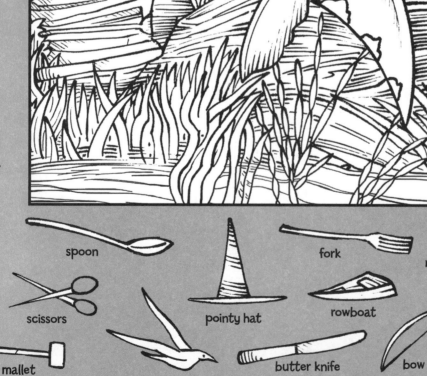

Art by Joe Seidita

drinking glass

spoon

scissors

mallet

pointy hat

seagull

fork

rowboat

butter knife

banana

bow

football

slice of cake

broom

tack

Jurassic Joy

heart

lollipop

wishbone

carrot

artist's brush

trowel

toothbrush

teacup

fork

baseball bat

mitten

drinking straw

pencil

mushroom

ruler

chili pepper

slice of pie

envelope

Art by Leighanne Schneider

T. rex and Triceratops

rabbit

bell

heart

clothespin

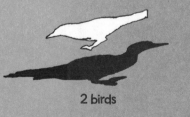
2 birds

duck

dolphin

rat

seal

snake

Art by Kit Wray

Field-Day Games

scissors

ice-cream cone

boomerang

ring

tack

banana

slice of pizza

matchstick

bacon

envelope

comb

mitten

ruler

croissant

Art by Neil Numberman

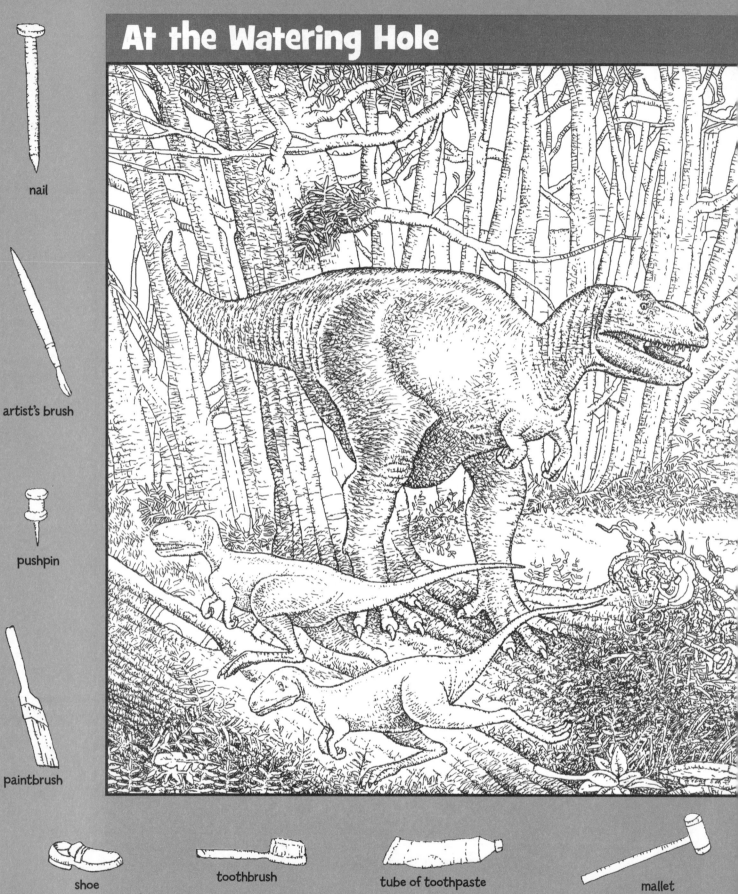

nail

artist's brush

pushpin

paintbrush

shoe

toothbrush

tube of toothpaste

mallet

slice of cake

flip-flop

pencil

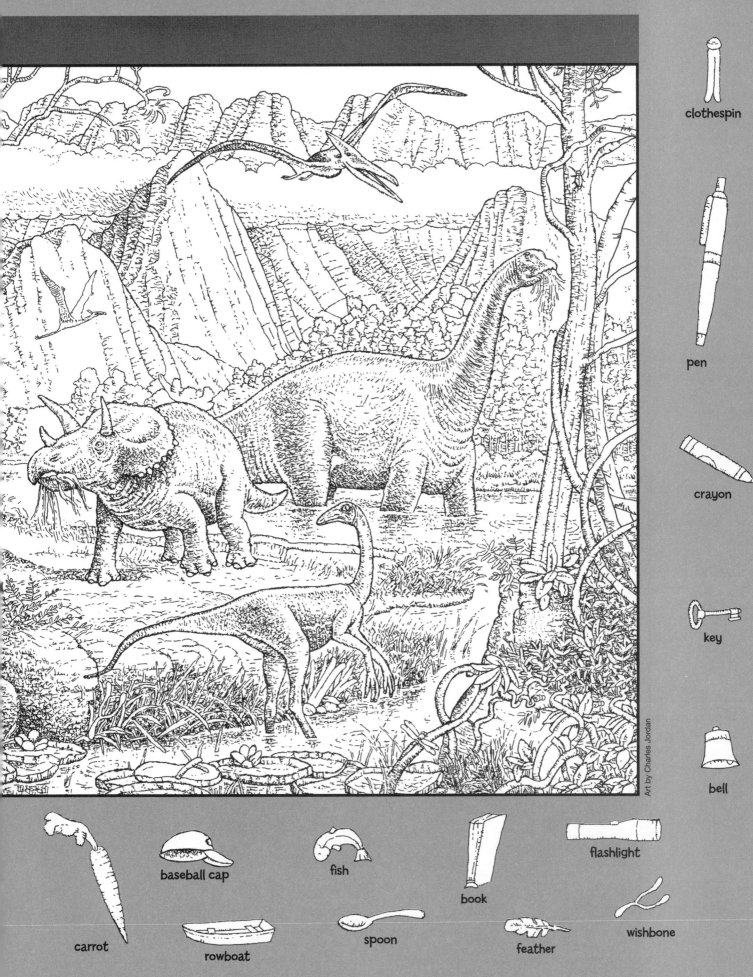

clothespin

pen

crayon

key

bell

carrot

baseball cap

rowboat

fish

spoon

book

feather

flashlight

wishbone

Art by Charles Jordan

Playful Dinosaurs

bowling ball

baseball bat

sock

olive

candy corn

domino

needle

star

heart

Art by Catherine Copeland

72

Discovering Dinos

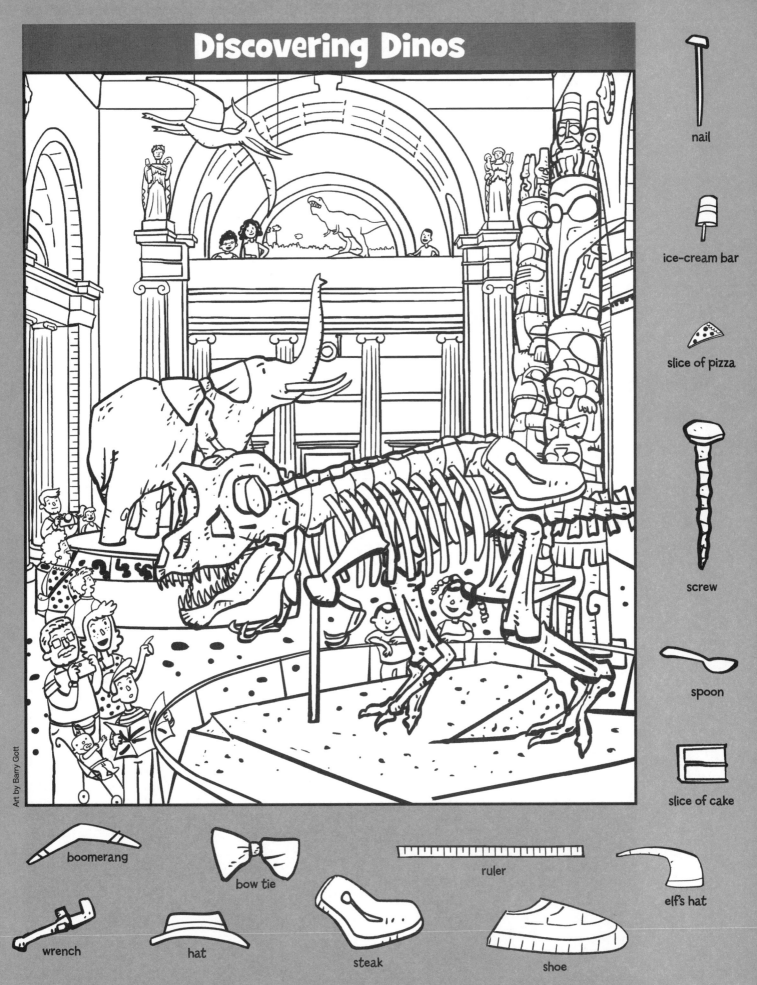

nail

ice-cream bar

slice of pizza

screw

spoon

slice of cake

boomerang

bow tie

ruler

elf's hat

wrench

hat

steak

shoe

Art by Barry Gott

73

Double Dutch

pennant

artist's brush

needle

candle

nail

musical note

ladle

golf club

toothbrush

banana

wishbone

heart

glove

comb

necktie

carrot

spoon

fish

pencil

Art by Mike DeSantis

Baby *Triceratops*

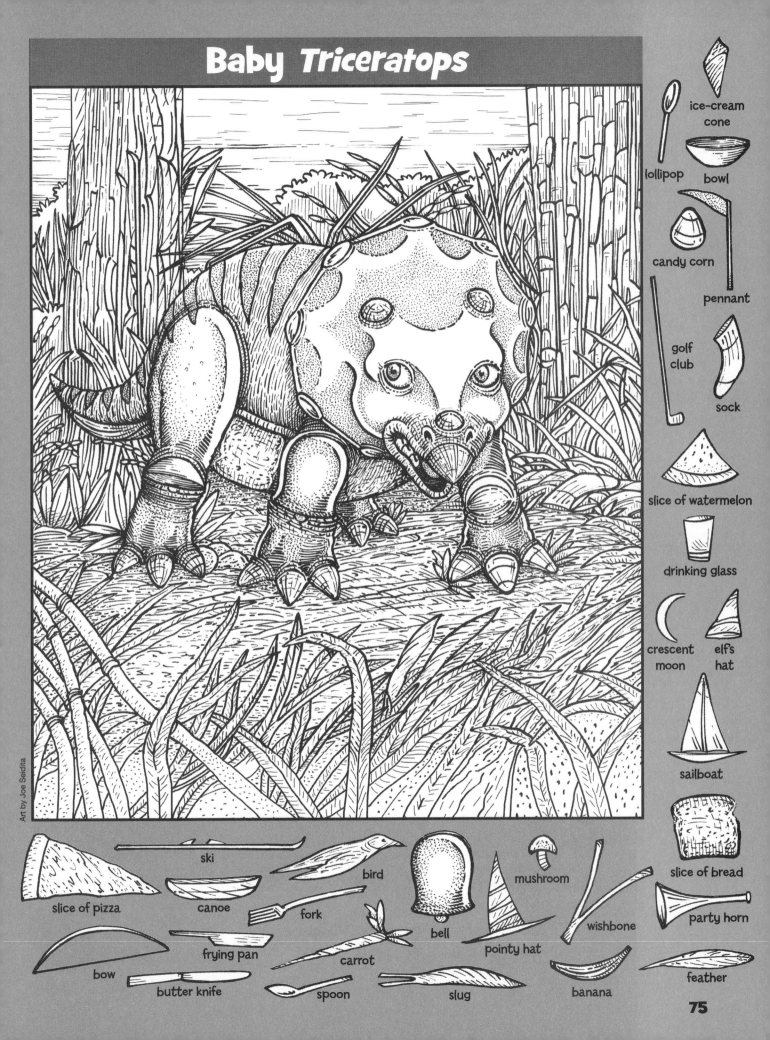

Art by Joe Seidita

ice-cream cone

lollipop

bowl

candy corn

pennant

golf club

sock

slice of watermelon

drinking glass

crescent moon

elf's hat

sailboat

slice of bread

ski

bird

slice of pizza

canoe

fork

mushroom

wishbone

party horn

bell

pointy hat

bow

frying pan

carrot

butter knife

spoon

slug

banana

feather

Pterodactyl Playtime

ice-cream bar

screwdriver

lollipop

hockey stick

flag

nail

pushpin

giraffe

sheep

canoe

sailboat

comb

Stegosaurus

teacup

cherry

pennant

NATURAL

glove

candle

golf club

carrot

hammer

domino

jar

pitcher

mushroom

pencil

sock

musical note

frying pan

toothbrush

mallet

slice of pie

lizard

spoon

magnet

teakettle

Art by Linda Weller

77

bee

bell

tweezers

needle

bowling ball

banana

safety pin

acorn

cherries

bird

scissors

artist's brush

hat

fish

Art by Lynn Adams

Welcome to the Museum

spool of thread

mushroom

banana

apple

bell

peanut

ladder

needle

button

flashlight

funnel

tube of toothpaste

Art by Rocky Fuller

79

Baby *Hadrosaurus*

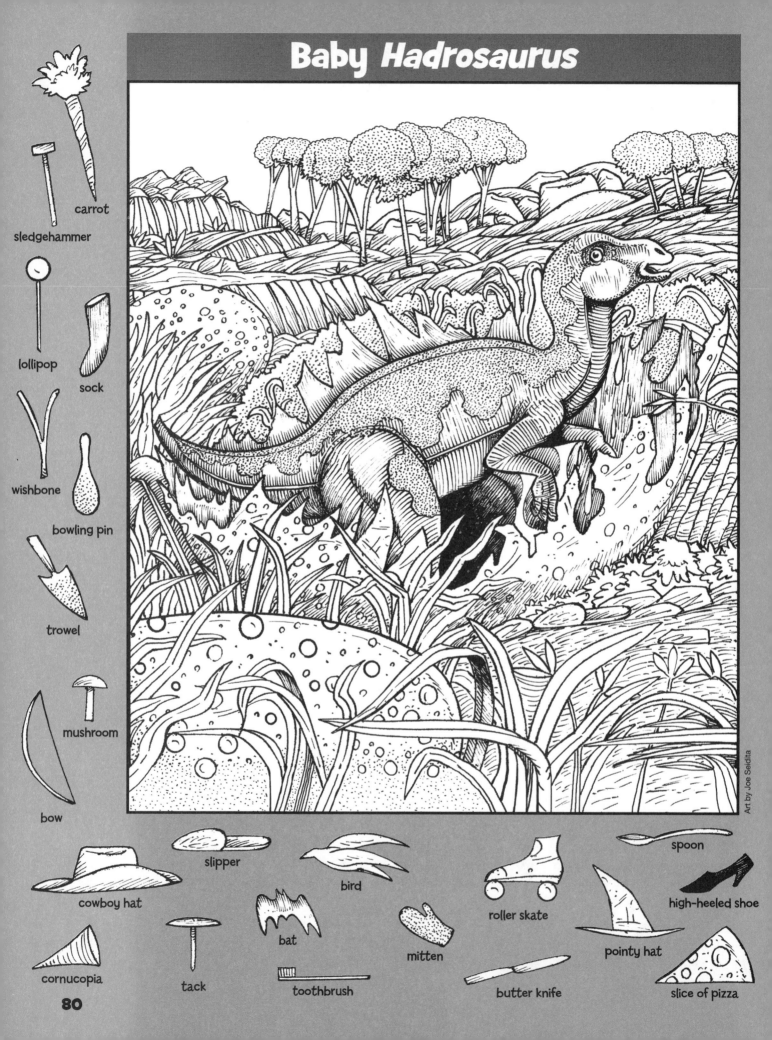

carrot

sledgehammer

lollipop

sock

wishbone

bowling pin

trowel

mushroom

bow

Art by Joe Seidita

cowboy hat

slipper

bird

roller skate

spoon

high-heeled shoe

cornucopia

tack

bat

mitten

butter knife

pointy hat

toothbrush

slice of pizza

On the Move

magic wand

umbrella

tack

bell

pushpin

candle

teacup

safety pin

flashlight

funnel

magnifying glass

sock

Art by Charles Jordan

Water-Balloon Battle

broccoli

yo-yo

snail

star

flag

mitten

ice-cream cone

wedge of lime

eggplant

saw

flowerpot

drum

Art by Beccy Blake

Jurassic Giants

fork

needle

screw

slice of bread

rabbit

mouse

dog's head

belt

bird

butter knife

heart

squirrel

A Trip to the Store

ice skate

butterfly

number 2

flashlight

ice-cream cone

teacup

eyeglasses

caterpillar

boot

bird

duck

mallet

clarinet

Art by Jill Droppa

worm

wrench

apple

crescent moon

golf club

ring

THE BIG DINO BOOK

SUN

toothbrush

flyswatter

heart

cracker

pennant

Triceratops Family

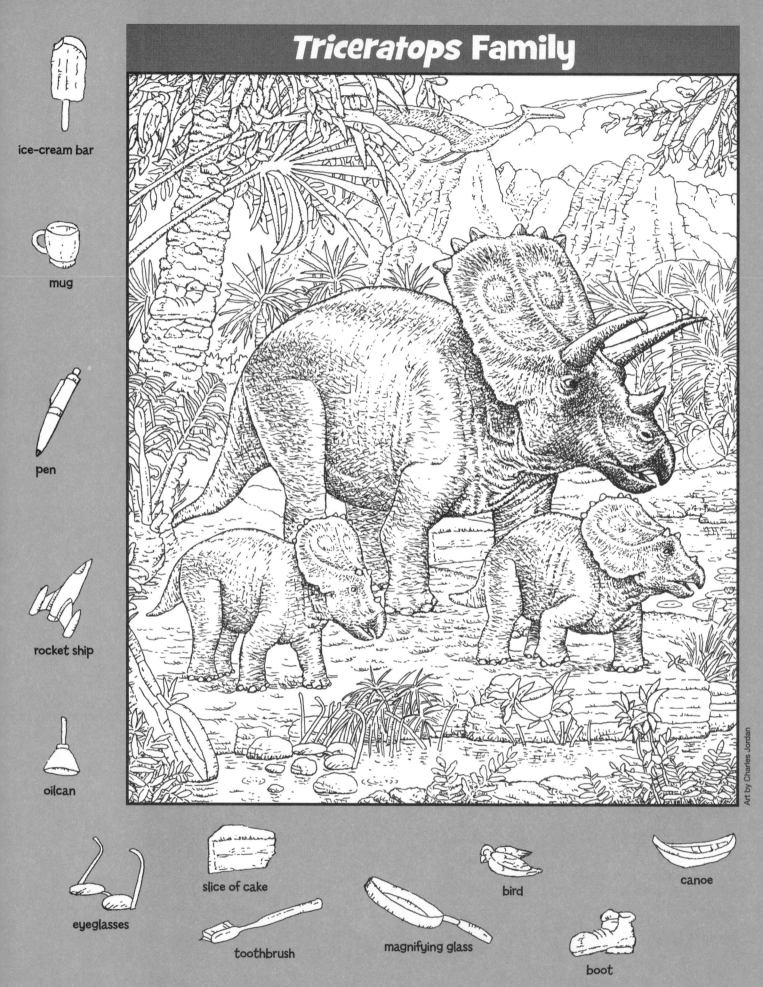

ice-cream bar

mug

pen

rocket ship

oilcan

eyeglasses

slice of cake

toothbrush

magnifying glass

bird

canoe

boot

88

Playtime

pennant

caterpillar

cane

golf club

carrot

tack

banana

paintbrush

heart

chili pepper

arrow

pencil

magnifying glass

sailboat

artist's brush

crown

ring

Art by Lyn Martin

A Dinosaur Display

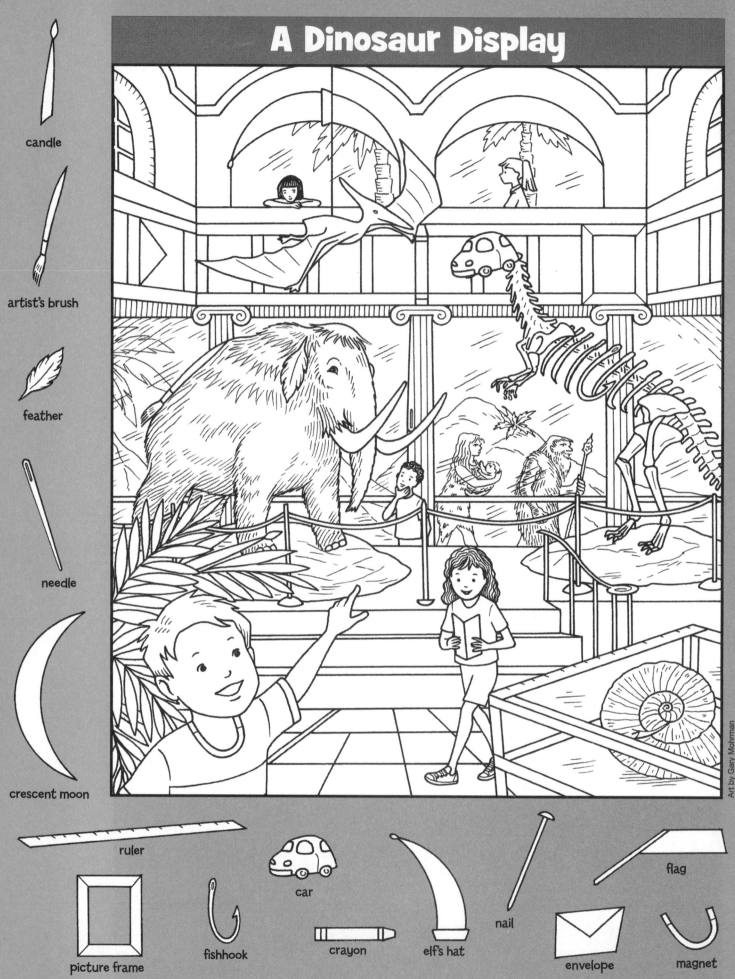

candle

artist's brush

feather

needle

crescent moon

ruler

picture frame

fishhook

car

crayon

elf's hat

nail

flag

envelope

magnet

Art by Gary Mohrman

Infant *Iguanodon*

Art by Joe Seidita

rocket ship

kite

boot

feather duster

hockey stick

elf's hat

ice-cream cone

spoon

wishbone

bat

slice of pizza

sponge

ship

princess hat

toothbrush

spoon

rabbit

canoe

candle

fish

slug

carrot

artist's brush

shark

fried egg

zipper

acorn

slice of pizza

hot dog

scissors

ladybug

pear

candle

fan

slice of bread

crown

Art by Beccy Blake

Bunny Paleontologists

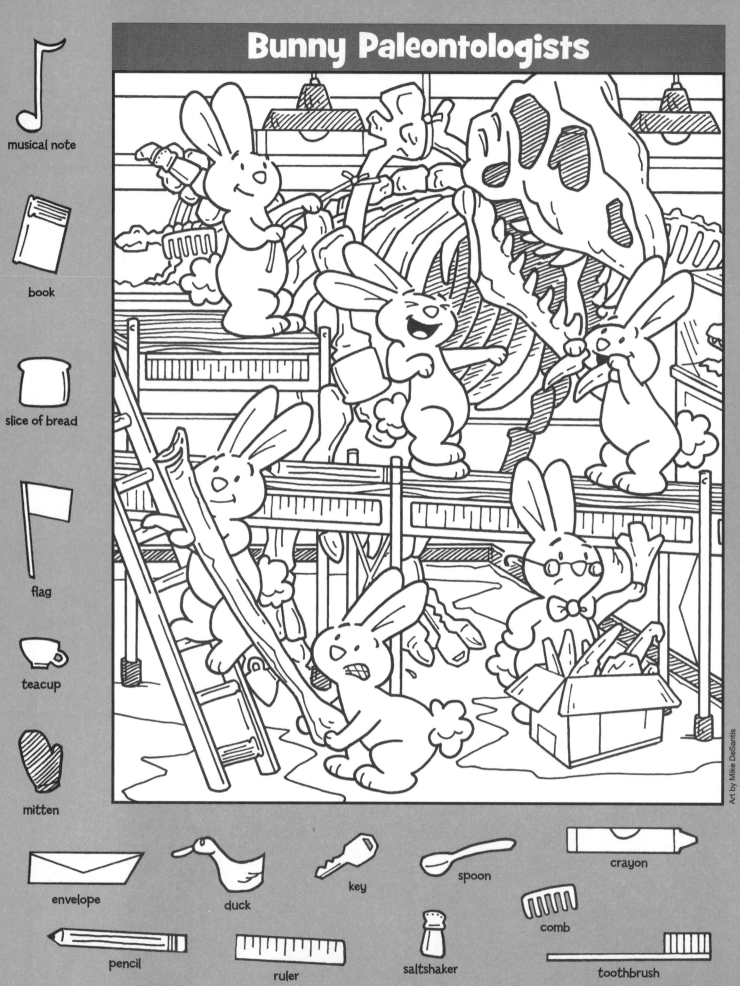

musical note

book

slice of bread

flag

teacup

mitten

envelope

duck

key

spoon

crayon

comb

pencil

ruler

saltshaker

toothbrush

Art by Mike DeSantis

Baby *Brachiosaurus*

Art by Joe Seidita

hockey stick

tack

ladle

butter knife

feather duster

carrot

ice-cream cone

artist's brush

rowboat

comb

frying pan

fish

shoe

pistachio nut

bird

feather

drinking glass

wishbone

pointy hat

slice of pizza

banana

slug

clarinet

fountain pen

carrot

bell

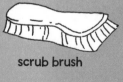
scrub brush

flashlight

half an apple

crayon

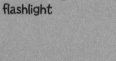
butter knife

gavel

slice of bread

96

Newborn *Diplodocus*

party hat

crescent moon

artist's brush

lollipop

hockey stick

ice-cream cone

kite

shoe

sailboat

archer's hat

slice of cake

carrot

snake

bird

fork

slice of pizza

pointy hat

coat hanger

ladle

football

cornucopia

butter knife

fried egg

Art by Joe Seldita

ghost

crescent moon

doughnut

hat

teapot

knitted hat

banana

fork

pine tree

dog

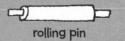
rolling pin

sheep

Art by Beccy Blake

Baby *Stegosaurus*

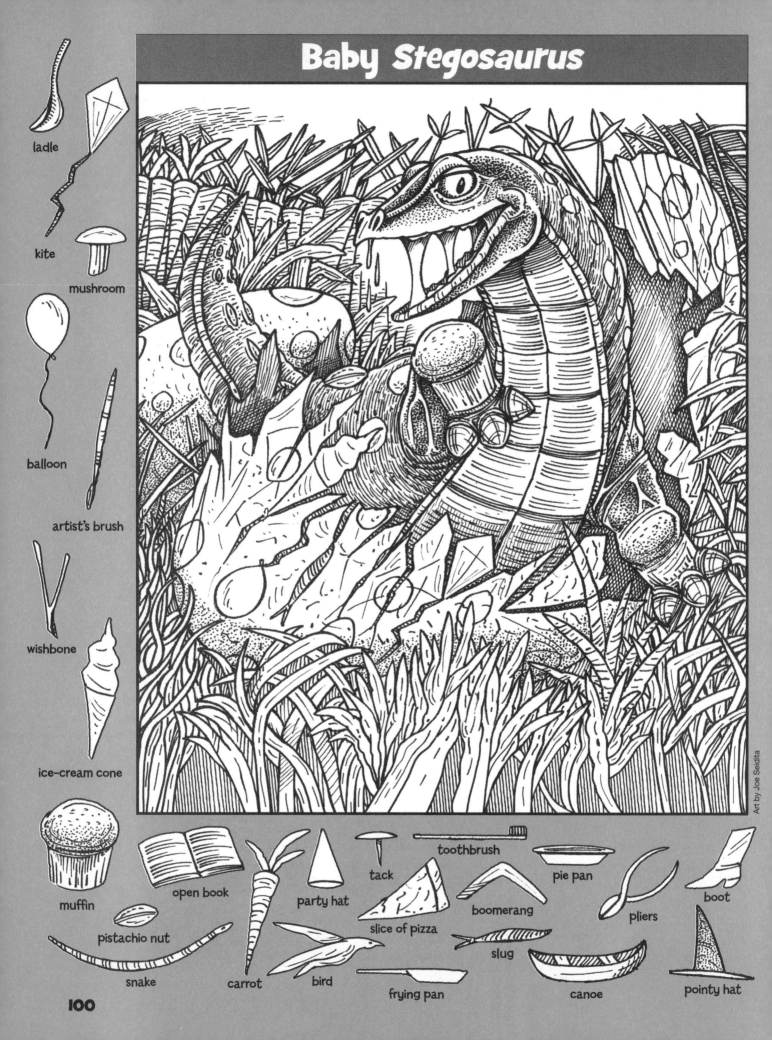

ladle

kite

mushroom

balloon

artist's brush

wishbone

ice-cream cone

muffin

open book

pistachio nut

snake

carrot

party hat

bird

tack

slice of pizza

toothbrush

boomerang

slug

frying pan

pie pan

pliers

canoe

boot

pointy hat

Art by Joe Seidita

Museum Visit

spool of thread

clothespin

banana

candle

slice of bread

bear

saw

button

baseball cap

mitten

bottle

domino

key

crown

saltshaker

toothbrush

Art by Maggie Swanson

Jump In!

cane

pointy hat

mallet

butter knife

candle

sailboat

baseball bat

bird

belt

mouse

glove

seal

spoon

Art by Kit Wray

New Friends

banana

star

fishing pole

horn

glove

crown

ladder

duck

peacock

eagle's head

fish

mouse

bull's head

Art by Tim Davis

Field Trip

paintbrush

bird

wristwatch

toothbrush

sock

teacup

drinking straw

nail

tube of toothpaste

spoon

fish

slice of pie

Art by R. Michael Palan

Dig This!

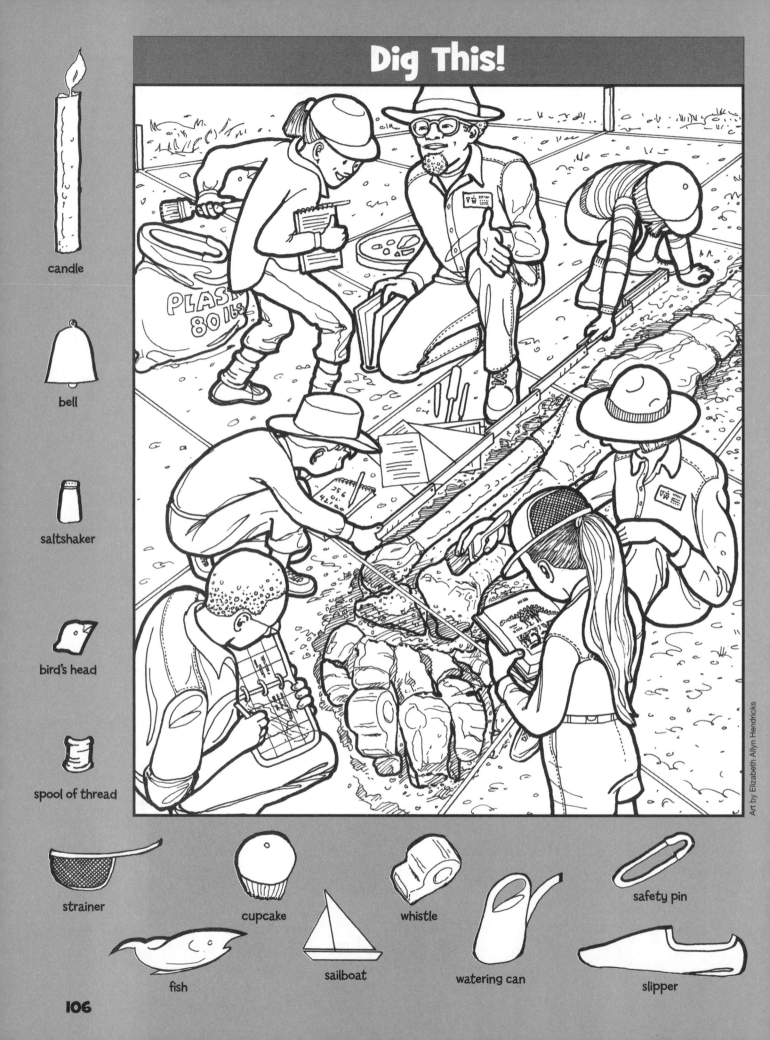

candle

bell

saltshaker

bird's head

spool of thread

strainer

cupcake

sailboat

whistle

watering can

safety pin

fish

slipper

Art by Elizabeth Allyn Hendricks

bell

glove

baseball bat

carrot

crown

heart

snake

pear

envelope

banana

comb

teacup

pencil

Snow Dino

fish

sock

candle

muffin

funnel

ghost

comb

feather

fishhook

pointy hat

crescent moon

ruler

seashell

teacup

star

Art by Gary Mohrman

108

ice-cream cone

glove

bow tie

butterfly

paper clip

pickle

kite

chili pepper

Art by Dave Clegg

Baby *Gallimimus*

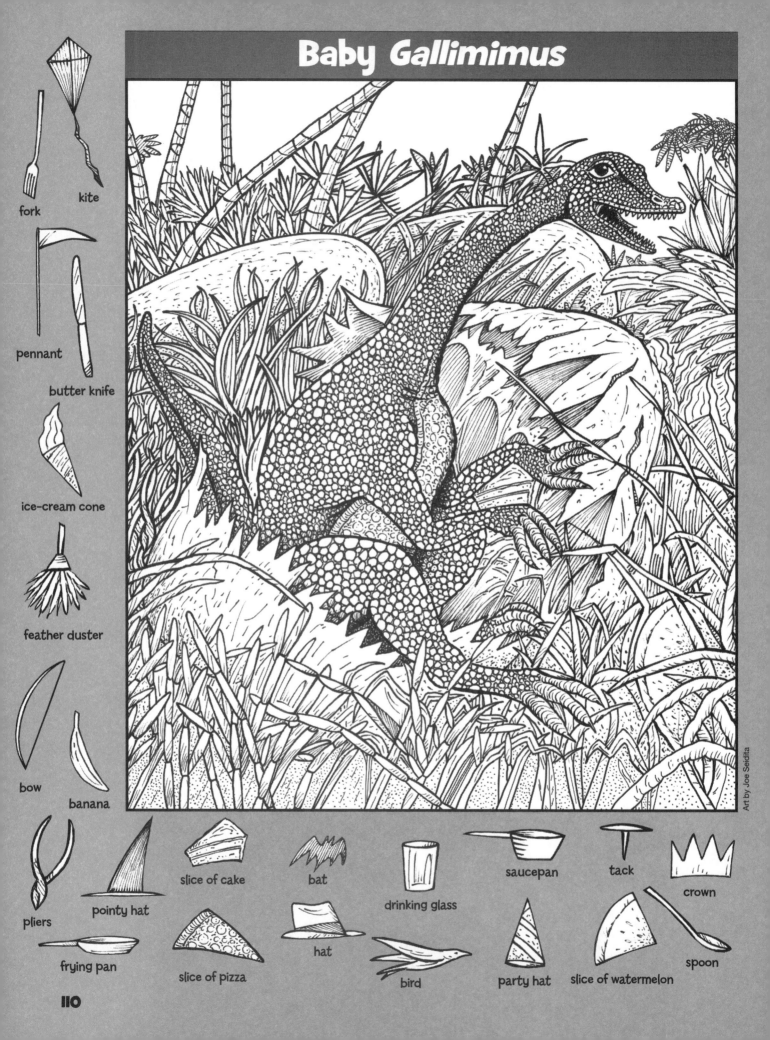

fork

kite

pennant

butter knife

ice-cream cone

feather duster

bow

banana

pliers

pointy hat

frying pan

slice of cake

slice of pizza

bat

hat

bird

drinking glass

saucepan

party hat

tack

slice of watermelon

crown

spoon

Art by Joe Seidita

Dino-soar!

cane

ice-cream cone

pennant

crescent moon

wishbone

hatchet

boomerang

rabbit

ring

shark

elf's hat

Art by Kit Wray

111

muffin

shoe

pencil

rake

baseball bat

bell

mitten

slice of pie

slice of bread

football

paper clip

rooster

feather

umbrella

sailboat

roller skate

house

spoon

fishhook

bugle

flashlight

Art by Kevin Rechin

Dino Land

football

acorn

olive

fried egg

slice of lime

snake

needle

boomerang

adhesive bandage

hot dog

cookie

binoculars

Art by Amy Schimler

114

Speedy Scooters

funnel

tack

golf club

candle

umbrella

paintbrush

mitten

flashlight

spatula

ice-cream cone

pushpin

safety pin

A Giant among Giants

rake

ant

owl

fish

fork

horse's head

sailboat

dog's head

eagle

rooster

cowboy hat

pig

lizard

squirrel

bird

hammer

candle

spoon

feather

penguin

seashell

Art by Kit Wray

lion's head

slice of pie

gorilla's head

loaf of bread

seal

snake

mouse

raccoon

walrus's head

rabbit

Fun at the Museum

recorder

pencil

cane

spoon

fish

squirrel

lollipop

envelope

bell

top hat

ice-cream bar

button

mitten

t-shirt

2 rabbits

crescent moon

baseball bat

banana

saltshaker

turtle

iron

boomerang

ornament

open book

needle

snake

drinking straw

tube of toothpaste

slice of pizza

Art by Karen Stormer Brooks

Tyrannosaurus rex

rabbit's head

pointy hat

glove

spoon

2 birds

crown

shark

eel

shoe

weasel

Art by Kit Wray

Dinosaur and Friends

flag

spoon

artist's brush

vacuum cleaner

baseball cap

golf club

rabbit

megaphone

scissors

question mark

dolphin

butterfly

house

pie

worm

tube of toothpaste

book

crown

Art by R. Michael Palan

That's Tall

baseball bat

hammer

ice-cream bar

fish

fried egg

ring

golf club

pencil

crescent moon

comb

toothbrush

carrot

Art by R. Michael Palan

Forest Fun

bow

whisk

drumstick

necktie

needle

whisk broom

pie

boomerang

football

peanut

jack

hat

stethoscope

bowling pin

artist's brush

baton

nail file

Art by Mark Corcoran

slice of cake

cherry

chef's hat

mitten

light bulb

ice-cream cone

pennant

125

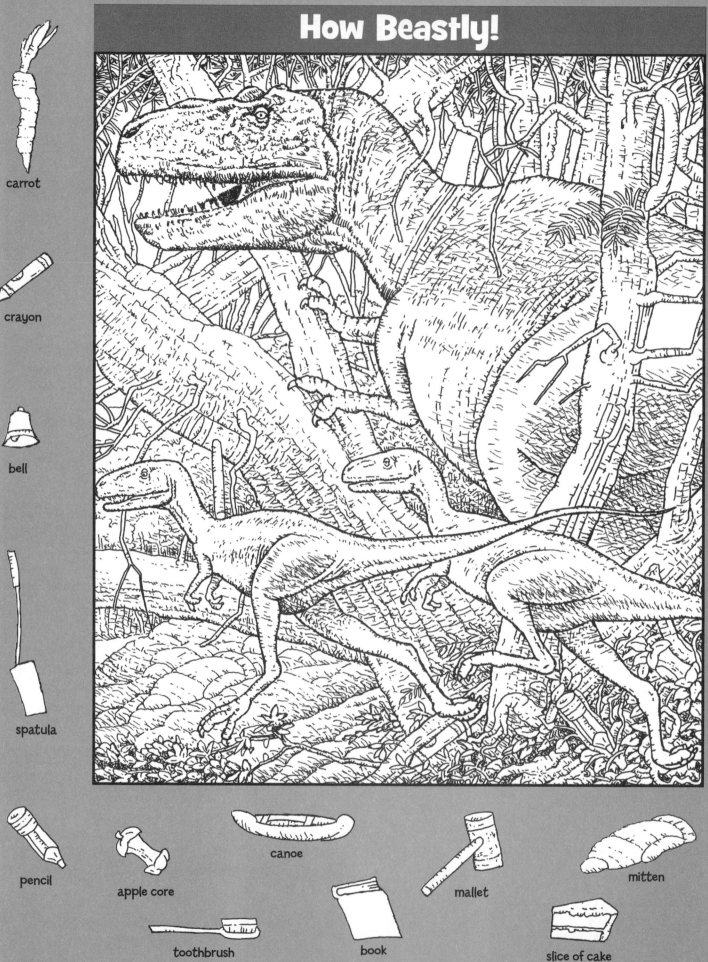

carrot

crayon

bell

spatula

pencil

apple core

canoe

toothbrush

book

mallet

slice of cake

mitten

Dinosaur Dash

hockey stick

hammer

ladle

baby's bottle

turtle

necktie

wristwatch

fish

light bulb

hat

boot

coat hanger

dog bone

bowl

Art by Jill Droppa

The Big Dig

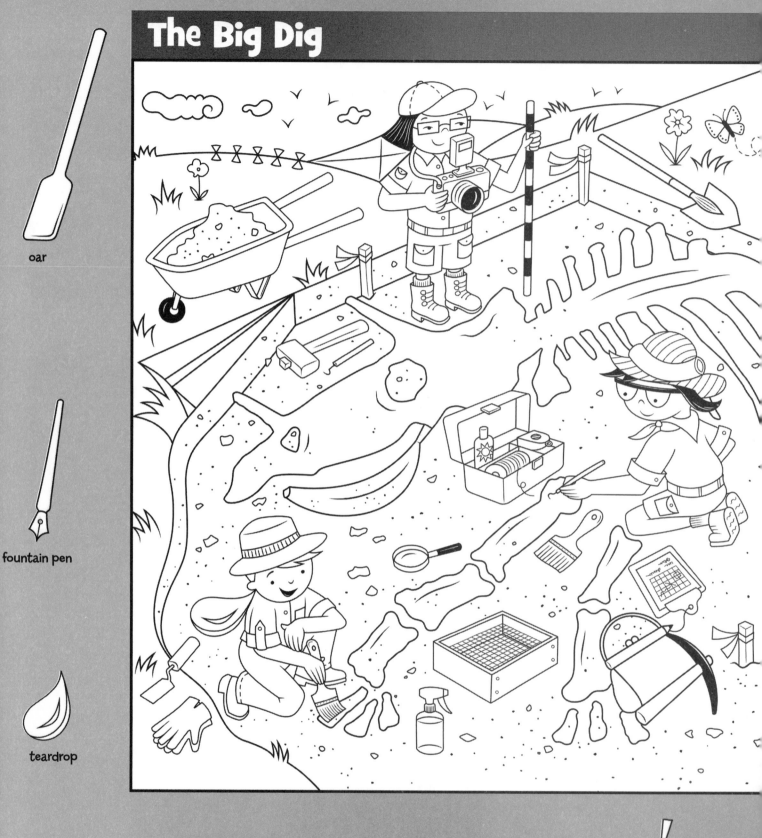

oar

fountain pen

teardrop

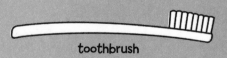
toothbrush

horseshoe

banana

artist's brush

kite

piece of popcorn

paper airplane

handbag

elbow noodle

Art by Christine Schneider

Answers

▼Pages 4-5

▼Page 6

▼Page 7

▼Page 8

▼Page 9

▼Pages 10-11

▼Page 12

▼ Page 13

▼ Page 14

▼ Page 15

▼ Pages 16-17

▼ Page 18

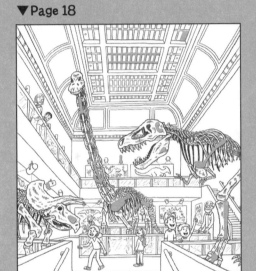

▼ Page 19

▼ Page 20

▼ Page 21

Answers

▼Pages 22

▼Pages 23

▼Page 24

▼Page 25

▼Page 26

▼Page 27

▼Pages 28-29

▼Page 30

Answers

▼Page 31

▼Page 32

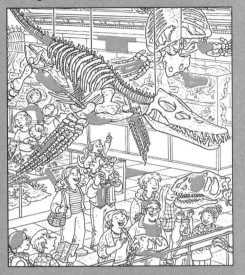

▼Page 33

▼Pages 34

▼Pages 35

▼Page 36

▼Page 37

▼Page 38-39

Answers

▼Pages 40-41

▼Page 42-43

▼Pages 44-45

▼Page 46

Answers

▼Page 47

▼Page 48

▼Page 49

▼Pages 50

▼Page 51

▼Page 52-53

▼Page 54

Answers

▼Pages 55

▼Pages 56

▼Page 57

▼Page 58

▼Page 59

▼Page 60

▼Page 61

▼Page 62

▼Page 63

▼ Pages 64–65

▼ Page 66

▼ Page 67

▼ Page 68

▼ Page 69

▼ Pages 70–71

▼ Page 72

Answers

▼Page 73

▼Page 74

▼Page 75

▼Pages 76-77

NATURAL HISTORY MUSEUM

▼Page 78

▼Page 79

▼Page 80

▼Page 81

▼Pages 82-83

▼Page 84

▼Page 85

▼Pages 86-87

▼Page 88

▼Page 89

▼Page 90

Answers

▼Page 91

▼Pages 92-93

▼Page 94

▼Page 95

▼Page 96

▼Page 97

▼Pages 98-99

▼Page 100

▼Page 101

▼Page 102

▼Page 103

▼Pages 104–105

▼Page 106

▼Page 107

▼Page 108

Answers

▼ Page 109

▼ Page 110

▼ Page 111

▼ Pages 112–113

▼ Page 114

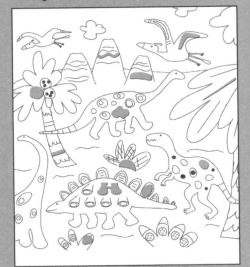

▼ Page 115

▼ Pages 116–117

▼Pages 118-119

▼Page 120

▼Page 121

▼Pages 122-123

▼Pages 124-125

▼Page 126

Answers

▼ Page 127

▼ Pages 128-129

For information about permission to reproduce
selections from this book, please contact
permissions@highlights.com.

Published by Highlights Press
815 Church Street
Honesdale, Pennsylvania 18431
ISBN: 978-1-62979-780-9
Manufactured in Secaucus, NJ, USA
Mfg. 08/2019

First edition
Visit our website at Highlights.com.
10 9 8 7 6